Taylor Swift

Iconic Music Industry Trailblazer

by Grace Hansen

Abdo Leading Biographies Kids

Abdo Kids Jumbo is an Imprint of Abdo Kids
abdobooks.com

abdobooks.com

Published by Abdo Kids, a division of ABDO, P.O. Box 398166, Minneapolis, Minnesota 55439.

Abdo Kids Jumbo™ is a trademark and logo of Abdo Kids.

Printed in the United States of America, North Mankato, Minnesota.

052024

092024

THIS BOOK CONTAINS RECYCLED MATERIALS

Photo Credits: AP Images, Getty Images, Shutterstock, ©fandom p.9,11,13,15,17,19/CC-BY-SA

Production Contributors: Teddy Borth, Jennie Forsberg, Grace Hansen
Design Contributors: Candice Keimig, Pakou Moua

Library of Congress Control Number: 2023948707

Publisher's Cataloging-in-Publication Data

Names: Hansen, Grace, author.

Title: Taylor Swift: iconic music industry trailblazer / by Grace Hansen

Description: Minneapolis, Minnesota : Abdo Kids, 2025 | Series: Leading biographies | Includes online resources and index.

Identifiers: ISBN 9798384900788 (lib. bdg.) | ISBN 9798384901488 (ebook) | ISBN 9798384901839 (Read-to-me eBook)

Subjects: LCSH: Swift, Taylor, 1989---Juvenile literature. | Women singers--United States--Biography--Juvenile literature. | Popular music--Juvenile literature. | Businesswomen--Biography--Juvenile literature. | Actors and actresses—Biography--Juvenile literature. | Women rock musicians--United States--Biography--Juvenile literature.

Classification: DDC 782.42163--dc23

Table of Contents

Taylor's Beginnings

Taylor Alison Swift was born on December 13, 1989, in West Reading, Pennsylvania. She grew up on a Christmas tree farm with her mom, dad, and younger brother Austin.

Pennsylvania
West Reading

By the age of 10, Taylor was performing at local talent shows. At 12, she began guitar lessons. She also wrote her first song, "Lucky You." Taylor dreamed of being a country music star.

The Swifts moved to Tennessee to support Taylor's dream. In 2006, Taylor joined a **record label** and got to work. Her first **single**, "Tim McGraw," hit radio stations in June. In October, she released her first full-length album *Taylor Swift*.

Taylor Swift
Taylor

To the Top

Taylor's second album *Fearless* **debuted** in November of 2008. It became the best-selling album of 2009. It also earned Taylor her first of many **Grammy** Awards.

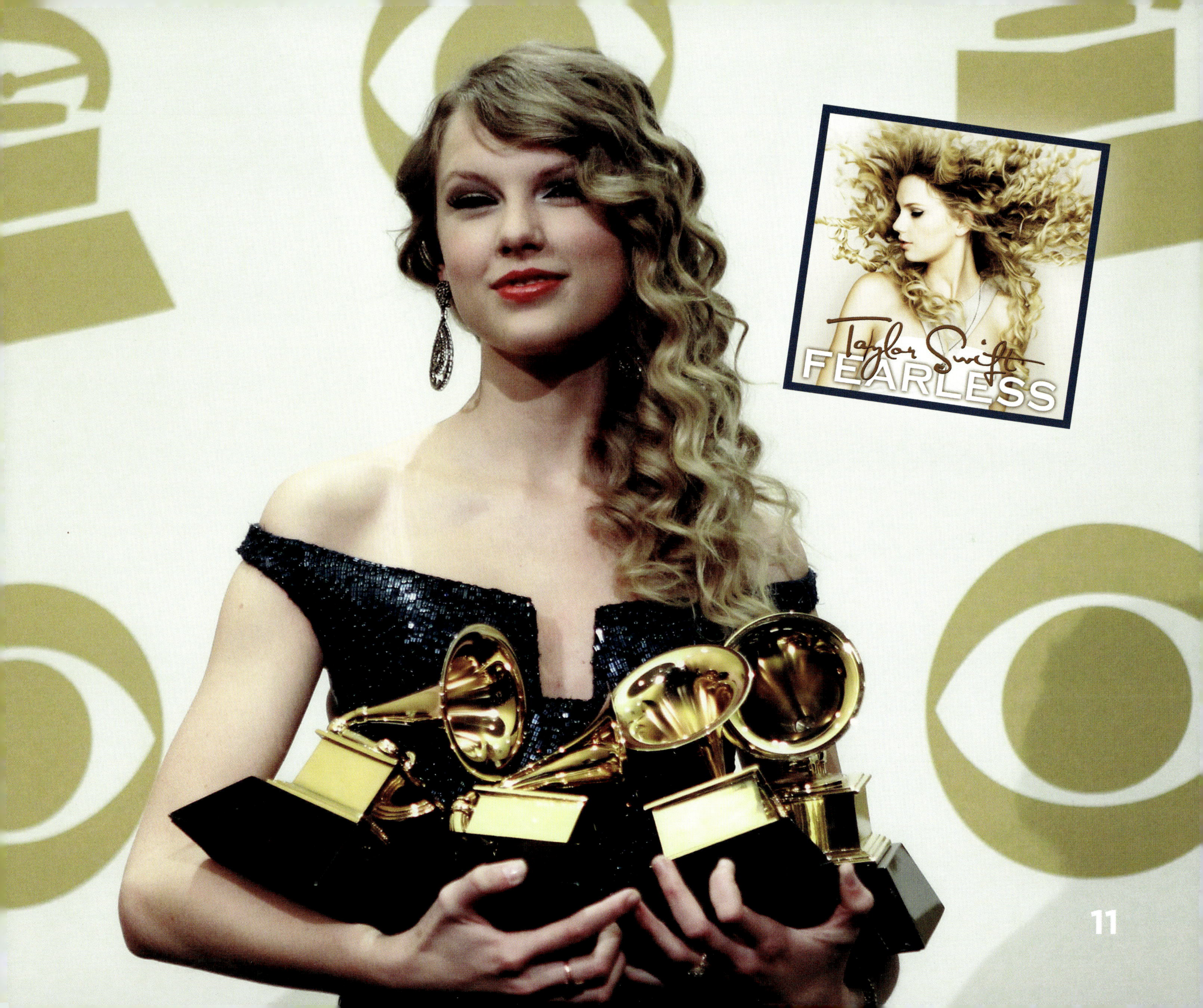
Taylor Swift
FEARLESS

Speak Now hit the shelves in October 2010. Two years later, Taylor released *Red*. The year 2014 marked a turning point in Taylor's career. Her pop album, *1989*, was her first big step away from country music.

Speak Now
Taylor Swift
RED
TAYLOR SWIFT
T.S. 1989

In 2015, Taylor began to struggle with fame. She stepped out of the spotlight but kept writing. In 2017, she released *Reputation*. **Critics** called it her best album yet. In August of 2019, the much lighter *Lover* album **debuted**.

reputation
Lover

Taylor released *Folklore* and *Evermore* just five months apart in 2020. Each album's mellow **ballads** told a story.

Taylor released her tenth studio album, *Midnights*, in 2022. The album broke many records. Soon after, Taylor announced The Eras Tour! The show would celebrate all of her musical **eras**.

Midnights
Lavender Haze
Maroon
Anti-Hero
Snow On The Beach
You're On Your Own, Kid
Midnight Rain
Question...?
Vigilante Shit
Bejeweled
Labyrinth
Karma
Sweet Nothing
Mastermind

More Eras to Come!

Taylor is a gifted songwriter and performer. The global superstar continues to surprise fans. Everyone is excited to see what Taylor does next!

SWIFT
S TOUR
TAYLOR SWIFT
THE ERAS TOUR
OCTOBER 13

Career Highlights

2004 Taylor signs her first publishing deal with Sony/ATV. She is the youngest signing in the company's history.

2010 Swift wins her first **Grammy** for Best Female Country Vocal Performance for her song "White Horse."

2016 Swift wins three Grammy Awards, including Album of the Year for *1989*.

2017 *Reputation* sells 1.2 million copies in its first week.

2019 Swift earns six American Music Awards for a record-breaking total of 28 AMAs. That number climbed to 40 by 2023.

2021 Taylor releases her first re-recorded album *Fearless (Taylor's Version)*.

2023 Taylor Swift is announced *Time* magazine's Person of the Year.

2024 Taylor Swift makes history as the first person to win the Grammy's Album of the Year award four times.

Glossary

ballad – a song that tells a story.

critic – a person whose work is to judge and write opinions about something such as music.

debut – to present to the public for the first time.

era – a period of time.

Grammy – any of various awards given annually in the US by the National Academy of Recording Arts and Sciences for outstanding achievement in music.

record label – a company that records and sells music.

single – a track released separately from an album.

Index